FOR YOUR HOME
LIGHTING IDEAS

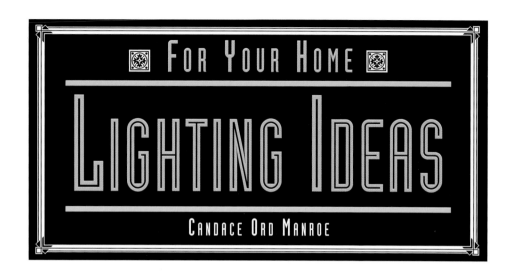

FOR YOUR HOME

LIGHTING IDEAS

CANDACE ORD MANROE

Little, Brown and Company

Boston   New York   Toronto   London

Dedication
For Meagan and Drew

First Edition

ISBN 0-316-54757-3

Library of Congress Catalogue Card Number 94-75952

A FRIEDMAN GROUP BOOK

10 9 8 7 6 5 4 3 2 1

Published simultaneously in Canada by Little, Brown & Company (Canada) Limited

FOR YOUR HOME: LIGHTING IDEAS
was prepared and produced by
Michael Friedman Publishing Group, Inc.
15 West 26th Street
New York, New York 10010

Editor: Sharyn Rosart
Art Director: Jeff Batzli
Designers: Patrick McCarthy and Lynne Yeamans
Photography Editor: Jennifer Crowe McMichael
Production Associate: Camille Lee

Color separations by Fine Arts Repro House Co., Ltd.
Printed and bound in China by Leefung-Asco Printers Ltd.

TABLE OF CONTENTS

INTRODUCTION: THE POWER OF LIGHT

The exceeding brightness of this early sun

Makes me conceive how dark I have

become,

And re-illumines things that used to turn

To gold in broadest blue....

The Sun This March, Wallace Stevens

After the dazzle of day is gone,

Only the dark, dark night shows to my eyes

the stars;

After the clangor of organ majestic,

or chorus, or perfect band,

Silent, athwart my soul, moves the

symphony true.

After the Dazzle of Day, Walt Whitman

Natural light—be it the first glimmer of sunshine breaking on the horizon, the fiery parade of color marching across the western sky at day's end, or the mysterious illumination within the black velvet of night—is the stuff of poetry. Light does more than make the external world visible: In its infinite variations, it tugs at the emotions, creating moods that range from heady exuberance to quiet introspection, even melancholy.

It isn't just natural light that carries such power. Artificial light, working independently or in tandem with natural light, has the same potential for affecting mood and eliciting an emotional response. Consider the magical effect of the flickering light cast by a candle-lit chandelier, the eerie illumination produced by a red bulb, or the soft glow that emanates from a Japanese paper lantern.

Left: THE SOFT FLICKER OF CANDLELIGHT IS THE MOST INTIMATE LIGHTING CHOICE AND ONE THAT SHOULD NOT GO OVERLOOKED WHEN HIGH-INTENSITY ILLUMINATION IS NOT NECESSARY. FOR DINING, CONSIDER A CANDLELIT CHANDELIER SUPPORTED BY THE WARM LIGHT FROM A COLLECTION OF CANDLESTICKS ON THE TABLE AND SIDEBOARD.

Given light's power, it's not surprising that in recent years lighting has risen dramatically in importance as a consideration, and a tool, in interior design. Until recently, lighting was considered a merely utilitarian concern, like plumbing or wiring; today, however, it is recognized as a design element of some importance. Along with color, pattern, traffic flow, and other fundamental design concerns, lighting is now being planned in the conceptual phase of home design, instead of being afterthought. An examination of a home's natural light sources—its windows, skylights, and French or atrium doors—is becoming as basic an undertaking as considering the home's palette and furniture style. The generic overhead room light, with its complement of tabletop lamps, though still viable, is no longer the automatic solution to lighting the home.

Instead, among savvy designers, architects, and do-it-yourself homeowners, lighting is being considered on a room-to-room, space-to-space basis, varying greatly from one place to the next depending upon the design goals. For example, in a room in which no single object or collection of *objets d'art* merits special attention, lighting may be diffused and moody, spreading a soft illumination throughout the space. In an area filled with beloved collectibles or art, the most effective lighting solution would be quite different, highlighting the desired objects with precise, direct light.

For a public space where a friendly feeling is desired, such as a family room, a traditional overhead fixture or chandelier might be the best artificial lighting choice, augmented by a vast wall of windows to bring in some welcome natural light. Even when the artificial lighting chosen is the standard overhead fixture, the room's mood can be changed by a device as simple and inexpensive as the reostat, or dimmer, which allows manipulation of the degree of light emitted.

In a highly architectural space, lighting, to realize its full potential, should underscore the architecture through a sophisticated blend of diverse light sources—a combination, perhaps, of up-, down-, and back-lights for evening,

Right: WHEN DESIGNING A HOME, THE PLACEMENT OF WINDOWS FOR TAKING ADVANTAGE OF NATURAL LIGHT AND VIEW SHOULD BE OF PRIME CONCERN. A SERPENTINE GLASS WALL IS INHERENT TO THE DESIGN STATEMENT OF THIS CONTEMPORARY HOME, DISSOLVING THE BOUNDARIES BETWEEN INDOORS AND OUTDOORS AND FLOODING THE SPACE WITH UNOBSCURED SUNSHINE.

with carefully situated skylights, windows, and glass doors to maximize the architectural beauty during the day.

Lighting can be given unusual applications. For example, a light placed inside the marble steps of a staircase would create a beautiful, translucent glow. Even staple lighting solutions such as lamps can vary greatly in impact and mood when carefully chosen: Handmade parchment shades or the thin, filmy paper of Japanese lanterns impart a soft, ethereal glow much different from that of a more opaque shade, which diverts the direction of the light downward. Victorian beads and fringe also work to dapple lamplight, creating more interesting patterns of shadow and light than are possible with a uniform fixture or shade. For a home in which budget permits lighting to become art in its own right, laser lights—which require installation by licensed specialists—can bathe planes of color across a surface or highlight desired objects with deft precision.

In the kitchen and bath, where the function of lighting is especially important for accomplishing tasks, the idea of a single overhead light source is being regarded, more and more, as antiquated and ineffective. Instead, such choices as recessed fluorescent down-lights are appearing as a means of illuminating kitchen countertop work spaces, while back-lights at the tops of cabinets provide an aesthetically

Above: IN THIS WET BAR, RECESSED DOWN-LIGHTS SHINE THROUGH GLASS SHELVES, SIMPLY AND EFFECTIVELY ACCENTUATING THE ATTRIBUTES OF THE GLASSWARE.

pleasing way of showing off groupings of pottery, baskets, crystal, or other collectibles. In the bathroom, lighting can take a theatrical turn, becoming bold, bright, and abundant—perhaps outlining an entire mirrored wall—for aid in accomplishing such light-dependent tasks as shaving or applying make-up.

Lighting within the home can create romantic or conversational moods, select focal points, announce formality or casual living, and cater to the specific tasks required of a space. In the end, lighting can change how a space looks and how those within it feel. Why, then, the delay in lighting becoming a full-fledged design tool, indispensable in the decorating process?

Lighting has been underutilized in home design for several reasons. First, lighting requires more pre-planning than do some other decorating tools. It's easier to settle for overhead fixtures and lamps—and ignore the thought of changing the number and size of windows—than it is to explore more effective lighting treatments that might require special wiring on structural changes before the room design can be implemented.

Second, lighting doesn't offer immediate and continual gratification, as do some other decorating elements such as furniture or color. To appreciate the effects of lighting, it is necessary to wait until the appropriate time of day or night when the lighting is at its best: A strategically placed skylight offers its most dramatic effects only when the sun is shining; lush, moody artificial lighting works its magic only when the sun has set.

Another reason lighting has been dismissed as a serious design issue is because it is contingent upon other objects within the design to accomplish its goal. Exquisitely backlit architectural niches achieve nothing, unless objects worthy of such dramatic lighting are displayed within them. (A cache of clutter or loose pocket change and car keys, under such lighting, makes the whole lighting enterprise appear superfluous or even ridiculous.) Similarly, the fine stream of sunshine spilling down from a entry hall skylight accomplishes little, unless the entry's architecture, flooring, and furnishings merit such illumination.

Finally, lighting hasn't received the attention it deserves because many homeowners simply feel inadequate, having little knowledge about the technicalities involved in beautifully lighting a home. Rather than becoming knowledgeable or calling in a professional, many homeowners have opted to ignore the lighting challenge altogether, settling for existing natural light and the usual artificial light sources.

In the following chapters, examples of innovative lighting solutions—both natural and artificial—will illustrate the uses of lighting as a design tool, encouraging readers to explore some of the ideas in their own homes. As the following examples demonstrate, lighting can enhance or completely change the perception of a home and the pleasure it provides, without requiring the replacement of a single piece of furniture. For the serious home decorator, lighting in all of its dimensions, both natural and artificial, has too much potential power to go unexplored.

THE NATURALS

In home design, lighting is a constant interplay between natural and artificial light, an ever-changing dynamic that unfolds over the course of a day. To thoroughly address lighting in the home, the appearance of the home's spaces must be considered at all times of day, from early morning to midday to late night, with as much attention paid to the effects of sunlight as to the result of strategically placed artificial lights.

During the day, a room with only a few small windows can appear dark and stuffy and elicit feelings of claustrophobia, or a sense of being uncomfortably disconnected from the natural environment. A relatively easy and inexpensive way to lighten the mood—both of the home and of those within it—is the addition of skylights.

Especially welcome in an interior room that is altogether devoid of windows and any natural light (as is sometimes the case with small guest bathrooms), a skylight is the obvious answer for opening up the space and

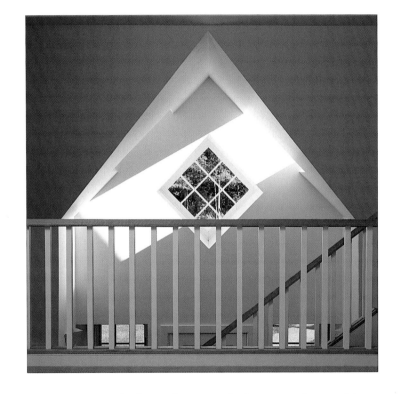

cheering it with the soft rays of the sun. Situated in a bedroom, above the bed, a skylight can have not only the daytime function of admitting golden light but the bonus of creating a romantic mood at night as well,

Above: Mimicking the architecture that surrounds it, a diamond-shaped, small-paned window at the top of a staircase washes the wall with jewel-like natural light during the day, calling attention to the architecture. By night, recessed lighting serves the same purpose. **Left:** Any pattern, color, window treatment, or art would be superfluous in this bedroom, which achieves its stellar good looks solely through its uniquely designed, arch-shaped combination of glass doors with contemporary interpretations of the fanlight and sidelights.

allowing stargazing before sleep, and on a good night, a restful slumber in gentle puddles of moonlight.

As a design tool, a skylight serves one other function: Like artificial lighting, it can create a focal point within a space. At the top of a staircase, for example, the sunlight filtering down through a skylight onto the stairs below calls attention to the architecture, showcasing the grain of the wood and the lines of the staircase wall as though these were works of art.

When conceptualizing an interior design, many professionals begin with the windows—not the window treatments, but the windows themselves. For it is the light in a room, more than the ornamentation, that can most dramatically change the appearance of a space. Increasing the size of windows, when doing so does not interfere with the home's architectural lines and character, is often among the first objectives of design.

Even when standard-size rectangular windows aren't feasible, cutting a small round or more unusual octagonal window in the wall can totally alter the space's look and mood. Even a small amount of natural light can warm up a room significantly. For imparting a feeling of oneness with nature, an entire wall of windows is a wise design solution, with the boundaries between indoors and outdoors seeming to dissolve due to the transparency of the walls. In such a space, the design goal is not about creating a mood of intimacy, but rather one of expansiveness.

The most romantic light source, candlelight, is a transition between natural and artificial light. In designing the home, candlelight should be considered as a frequently used light source, not one that is merely occasionally introduced over a romantic dinner for two. The creative use of candles from candlelit chandeliers and sconces to permanent groupings of candlesticks on tabletops can create a wonderful ambience unlike that of either natural or artificial light. A similar feeling can be created with the flickering flames of oil lamps and lanterns.

Artificial lighting doesn't have to look artificial. Some of the most interesting interpretations emulate nature. Down-lights, whether spotlights or floodlights, can produce shafts of light akin to sunshine pouring through a window. Strands of tiny white lights encircling a room create the effect of a nighttime sky. Japanese paper lanterns emit a subtle, quiet glow akin to moonlight.

When planning lighting for the home, it's wise to keep in mind the origins of light, working closely with nature for the best results.

Above: A GLASS-BLOCK WALL SURMOUNTED BY SKYLIGHTS PROVIDES A CREATIVE SOLUTION TO THE PROBLEM OF ADMITTING NATURAL LIGHT WHILE STILL RETAINING PRIVACY, AND PRECLUDES THE NEED FOR DECORATIVE WINDOW TREATMENTS. FILTERED THROUGH THE GLASS BLOCKS, THE LIGHT'S INTERESTING PATTERNS ARE FURTHER ACCENTUATED BY THE OPEN-GRID STAIRWAY RAILING.

Above: BREATHTAKING RESULTS REWARD BUILDERS WHO GET TO KNOW THEIR SITE, THEN DESIGN THE HOME ACCORDINGLY, WITH WINDOWS PLACED TO CAPTURE THE MOST DRAMATIC PRESENTATIONS OF BOTH MORNING AND EVENING LIGHT. PROOF IS THIS SUNSET VISTA WITH ITS RICH COLORATION, ANTICIPATED IN THE PLANNING STAGES OF THE HOME, THAT COORDINATES WITH AND COMPLETES THE INTERIOR PALETTE. **Left:** AN UNDER-THE-EAVES LOFT BEDROOM ATTAINS A PRISTINE NATURAL BEAUTY WITH THE BENEFIT OF A SINGLE ROUND WINDOW, CUT IN THE CENTER OF THE WALL JUST ABOVE THE BED.

Above: AN UP-LIGHT CREATES A MOODY EFFECT AKIN TO NATURAL, DAPPLED LIGHT WHEN SHONE UPON A PEDESTAL AND SCULPTURE. THE LIGHT IS POSITIONED SO THAT THE ILLUMINATION ASCENDS THE PEDESTAL TO REACH THE SCULPTURE, CREATING AN EFFECT THAT IS MUCH MORE INTRIGUING THAN THAT OF A DOWN-LIGHT SHINING DIRECTLY UPON THE SCULPTURE ITSELF. **Right:** FLOOR-TO-CEILING WOOD SCREENS WITH A CANE-LIKE GRID PATTERN DISSIPATE THE HARSHNESS OF DIRECT SUNLIGHT AND CREATE PRIVACY WHEN PLACED BEFORE THE WINDOWS. THEY STILL PERMIT SUNLIGHT INTO THE ROOM, HOWEVER, THROWING IT INTO LATTICEWORK SHAPES OF LIGHT AND SHADOW ON THE FLOOR AND FURNISHINGS.

Above: WHEN ARCHITECTURE TAKES A VERTICAL EXPRESSION WITH AN EMPHASIS ON SOARING CEILINGS, A DARK, CAVERNOUS FEELING CAN RESULT. THIS ROOM CIRCUMVENTS THE PROBLEM WITH EXPANSES OF GLASS ON TWO WALLS THAT RISE ALL THE WAY TO THE CEILING, BATHING THE ROOM IN NATURAL LIGHT THAT CREATES AN AIRY, CHEERFUL ATMOSPHERE.

Below: TO TRULY ADDRESS LIGHTING WHEN DESIGNING A SPACE, IT IS NECESSARY TO CONSIDER BOTH NATURAL AND ARTIFICIAL LIGHT IN TANDEM. THIS SPECTACULAR BATHROOM DESIGN SUCCEEDS IN USING LIGHT TO CREATE A DRAMATIC AMBIENCE: BY DAY, IT IS BATHED IN NATURAL LIGHT; BY NIGHT, RECESSED UP-LIGHTS AND DIRECTED DOWN-LIGHTS PROVIDE ILLUMINATION.

Below: WITH ITS LONGEST WALL DEVOID OF WINDOWS, THIS GALLEY-SHAPED BATHROOM MIGHT HAVE BEEN A STUDY IN DARKNESS. INSTEAD, THE ROOM IS WARMED BY SUNLIGHT STREAMING FROM SKYLIGHTS THAT SPAN THE ENTIRE LENGTH OF THE SPACE AND GLASS-BLOCK CORNER WALLS THAT ALLOW LIGHT INTO THE ROOM WITHOUT COMPROMISING THE NEED FOR PRIVACY. WITH THE NATURAL LIGHT AUGMENTED BY RECESSED DOWN-LIGHTS, THE BATHROOM THOROUGHLY ADDRESSES THE UTILITARIAN NEED FOR ADEQUATE LIGHTING TO PERFORM THE GROOMING TASKS ASSIGNED TO THE SPACE.

Above: NARROW SHAFTS OF LIGHT AND SHADOW CREATE A DAZZLING EFFECT IN THIS BATHROOM, IN WHICH A WIDE SKYLIGHT IS COVERED WITH CUSTOM-DESIGNED RATTAN BLINDS. THE STRIPED DESIGNS PRODUCED BY LIGHT FILTERING THROUGH THE BLINDS FALL ON VIRTUALLY EVERY SURFACE, INCLUDING THE WALLS, DOOR, AND TILE FLOOR.

Above left: As arteries between major living areas of the home, hallways are often sequestered from exterior walls, existing merely as dark and unappealing appendages. In this home, however, skylights make this passageway an aesthetic gem, dotting it with an interplay of light and shadow. **Above right:** The "eyes" of the home, windows are the feature to which we naturally gravitate. When conceived as a focal point of the design rather than as a staple element included by habit, a bank of windows can not only saturate a space with light but actually frame the outside view as though it was a work of art. **Right:** In a home in which the interior spaces ramble without access to exterior walls, a panel of skylights dominating the ceiling is an ideal solution for opening up the space and gracing it with welcome natural light.

Below: TINY DOWN-LIGHTS ILLUMINATE A DARK WOOD CEILING LIKE STARS IN A NIGHTTIME SKY. ARTIFICIAL LIGHTING'S EMULATION OF NATURE IS COMPLETED BY A GLOBE FIXTURE THAT HANGS LIKE A FULL MOON AMID THE SCATTERED PINPOINTS OF LIGHT.

Above: A PINT-SIZE KITCHEN WITHOUT WINDOWS RECEIVES SAVING GRACE FROM A SKYLIGHT GRID CENTRALLY PLACED IN THE ROOM. THE KITCHEN'S TRANSFORMATION FROM MERELY SALVAGEABLE TO HAVING ONE-OF-A-KIND STYLE IS COMPLETED BY A GLASS-BLOCK PANEL IN THE FLOOR THAT MIRRORS THE SKYLIGHT GRID OVERHEAD, REFLECTING ITS LIGHT.

Below: STRATEGIC PLACEMENT OF WINDOWS IS IMPORTANT FOR IMBUING A ROOM WITH THE APPROPRIATE AESTHETIC FEELING. THIS BATHROOM DERIVES ITS CHARACTER FROM THE BEAUTIFULLY PANED WINDOW THAT IS THE SPACE'S FOCAL POINT. POSITIONED AT THE TUB, THE WINDOW PERMITS CRISP MORNING LIGHT TO ENHANCE THE PLEASURE OF THE DAILY ROUTINE OF A SHOWER OR BATH.

Above: WHEN CREATIVITY IS GIVEN AS MUCH LICENSE IN THE DOMAIN OF LIGHTING AS IT IS IN OTHER DECORATING CONCERNS, THE EFFECT MAY BE AN UNEXPECTED AND WONDERFUL TURN OF FANCY, AS SEEN IN THIS BATHROOM. ITS WINDOWS ARE LARGELY DECORATIVE, BUT A MIRROR WITH STAINED-GLASS INSERTS THAT IS WRAPPED IN STRANDS OF TINY WHITE LIGHTS BRINGS BOTH ILLUMINATION AND A FESTIVE FLAIR TO THE SPACE.

Above left: PAPER LANTERNS POSSESS A SUBTLE, MOODY LUMINOSITY THAT IS AKIN TO MOONLIGHT ON WATER, IMPARTING A SERENE AND ROMANTIC FEELING THAT PRECLUDES THE NEED FOR MANY OTHER DECORATIVE ELEMENTS OR EVEN FURNISHINGS.

Above right: EVEN CONTEMPORARY LIGHT FIXTURES CAN CAPTURE THE ROMANCE OF CANDLELIGHT, AS SEEN BY THIS METAL AND GLASS PLATFORM CHANDELIER THAT IS HOST TO AN ARRAY OF VOTIVE CANDLES. THE SIMPLE BEAUTY OF THE VOTIVES IS REPEATED ON THE MANTELSHELF. **Left:** A SERIES OF IDENTICAL, DEEPLY RECESSED, SIMPLE RECTANGULAR WINDOWS POSITIONED NEAR THE CEILING ON TOWERING WALLS SCATTER SUNLIGHT ALONG THE CROWN OF THE ROOM—LIGHT THAT IS THEN REFLECTED ON THE DARK-STAINED CEILING FOR A MIRRORED EFFECT. THE SIMPLICITY AND FORM OF THE WINDOWS COMPLEMENT THE SPARE, LINEAR ARCHITECTURE OF THE SPACE.

Above: ANTIQUE LANTERNS NOT ONLY MAKE AN APPEALING COLLECTION, BUT WHEN LIT *EN MASSE*, AS IN THIS SHELVING NICHE, THEY PROVIDE AN INTRIGUING LIGHT SOURCE THAT DRAWS ATTENTION TO THE COLLECTION ITSELF. **Right:** LIKE CONSTELLATIONS, CIRCLES OF SPARKLING DOWN-LIGHTS IN THIS DINING ROOM BRING AN ETHEREAL NIGHTTIME MOOD TO THE DINING EXPERIENCE. THE ONLY OTHER LIGHT SOURCE NEEDED IS AN ELEGANT CANDELABRA.

Selective Interests

Evenly dispersed light is flat—and dull. Without the shape and dimension created by areas of shadow or the contrast of bright and dim light, a room has little dynamic appeal. This holds true with both natural and artificial light. When morning sunlight filters through a window, it is the dappled effect that provides emotional appeal and visual interest. In an artificially lit room at night, it is the contrast of more and less illuminated surfaces that strikes a mood.

In planning lighting for the home, then, it's important to be selective—to determine which areas merit the most illumination and which are better falling into shadow. A simple, effective approach to lighting begins by taking inventory of the spaces and objects within a room: Decide which areas have the most interesting architecture and which objects would best serve as focal points.

Once this has been determined, add light accordingly by putting skylights over beautiful, serpentine plaster

Above: Architectural in nature, these tall contemporary floor lamps are given unusual application at the windowsill, their up-lights illuminating the tiled ceiling above instead of the furnishings below. **Left:** Spotlights on tracks above the work centers of this kitchen add a contemporary feel to the room design, which is a mix of rustic and clean-lined. By their precise location, the fixtures also perform the utilitarian function of illuminating those specific areas in greatest need of light.

walls; adding tiny pinpoints of artificial down-lights to call attention to worthy collectibles or art; placing recessed down-lights beneath cabinets or entertainment-center shelving to fall softly on the objects below; or situating back-lights within shelving to mysteriously highlight displays of glassware, crystal, or minerals.

Canister up-lights create exquisite effects on otherwise bare walls, on *objets d'art*, or even on plants, throwing shadows from the ficus tree against the wall in a mottled pattern similar to the lacy quality of shadows created by sunlight itself. Shining through a glass table or pedestal, up-lights add a diffused, moody quality of romance and mystery to a room. Track lighting with floodlights creates a gallery effect, leaving little mistake about the importance of the objects benefiting from this high-intensity illumination. Fluorescent lights inset under a cabinet to illuminate a work space or the objects below achieve yet a different look, creating a diversity that adds to the overall visual interest of the space.

The most successful lighting solutions are those most closely tailored to fit the other elements in the home's design. In a dining room, for instance, it may be understood that the area deserving attention as the key light source is the space above the dining table. If the dimensions and shape of the dining table are known before the lighting is installed, lighting can be adapted to blend harmoniously with the furniture. A large, round table, for example, might be lit by a circle of recessed down-lights of a similar circumference, placed directly above the space designated for the table. If other furnishings in the room are identified, secondary light sources can be planned to complement those objects—with up-lights to bring a soft, patterned glow to plants and small spotlights to accentuate works of art. For the most dynamic design, try lighting the home with a number of different light sources of varying intensities and qualities.

Lighting the home is a matter of prioritizing, determining which areas should be highlighted and which can recede, or identifying a primary light source augmented by secondary sources. Then it's all creativity, using your imagination to shed the most effective or evocative light on the scene.

Right: Architecture and lighting go hand in hand, one reinforcing the other's effects. In this upper-story space, the abstract architectural planes are outlined by indirect lighting inset into the negative spaces of the configurations.

Left: SCONCES SHINE LIGHT UP ABOVE THIS ROOM'S PANELED WALLS UPON ITS RICHLY LACQUERED MOLDINGS, MAKING THEM SHIMMER LIKE DARK POOLS OF WATER IN THE SOFT ILLUMINATION. INDIVIDUAL LAMPS ARE USED WHEN MORE ILLUMINATION IS REQUIRED.

Right: IN A TRADITIONAL HOME THAT BOASTS AN IMPORTANT ART COLLECTION, THE ELEGANCE OF CRYSTAL SCONCES IS NOT ENOUGH. EACH PAINTING MERITS A LIGHT OF ITS OWN, IN ORDER TO RECEIVE FULL RECOGNITION AMID THE DISPLAY OF OPULENCE.

Above left: UP-LIGHTS INSET BEHIND CROWN MOLDING IN A GAP BETWEEN THE CEILING AND WALLS PROVIDE A GENTLE, UNUSUAL LIGHT FOR THIS DINING ROOM, AN ALTERNATIVE OR ADDITIONAL LIGHT SOURCE TO THE CONTEMPORARY CHANDELIER ABOVE THE TABLE. **Above right:** BEFORE PLANNING HOW TO LIGHT A ROOM, IT IS NECESSARY TO DETERMINE THE FOCAL POINT OF THE SPACE. IN THIS DINING ROOM, THE TABLE AND ADJACENT ART ARE HIGHLIGHTED BY DIRECTIONAL DOWN-LIGHTS MOUNTED ON A CEILING PLATFORM. PEEKING AROUND THE PERIMETER OF THE PLATFORM IS A SOFTER, DIFFUSED LIGHT THAT GIVES THE ENTIRE SPACE A MUTED GLOW.

Above: THE MORE SERIOUS THE HOME CHEF, THE MORE IMPORTANT LIGHTING BECOMES IN THE KITCHEN. HERE, WINDOWS AND SKYLIGHTS LET IN DAYLIGHT, WHILE A SUCCESSION OF FLOODLIGHTS ILLUMINATES KEY WORK SPACES, AND COMPATIBLE TRACK LIGHTING PROVIDES A MORE UNIFORM LIGHT ON STORAGE SPACES.

Right: RECESSED SPOTLIGHTS CAN BE PRECISELY DIRECTIONAL, PINPOINTING ILLUMINATION DOWN UPON KEY AREAS. IN THIS SERENE BEDROOM, SPOTS SHINE DIRECTLY ON THREE WORKS OF ART.

Above left: ADVANCE PLANNING IS ESSENTIAL IN ACHIEVING THIS SUBTLE YET HIGHLY DRAMATIC BACKLIGHTING ON GLASS SHELVES OF *OBJETS D'ART.* NOTE THE INTEREST CREATED BY THE CONTRAST IN TONE BETWEEN THE GOLDEN TUBE LIGHT AND THE SOFTER BLUE-GREEN BACK-LIGHTS. **Above right:** A SMALL, RECESSED DOWN-LIGHT ILLUMINATES THIS POWDER ROOM FROM ABOVE, WHILE A PAIR OF TUBE LIGHTS FLANKING THE MIRROR EFFECTIVELY PROVIDE THE BRIGHT CLARITY NECESSARY TO MAKE THE ROOM FUNCTIONAL. **Right:** LAMPLIGHT AND A DOUBLE-GLOBE SCONCE DRAW THE EYE TO THIS CHARMING BEDSIDE STILL LIFE OF PHOTOGRAPHS, CHINA, AND FLOWERS.

Above: A COMMON MISTAKE IN LIGHTING A ROOM IS TO ASSUME THAT DOWN-LIGHTS MUST BE CENTRALLY PLACED TO SHED LIGHT ACROSS THE ENTIRE SPACE. A MORE INTERESTING SOLUTION IS TO POSITION THEM SELECTIVELY, AS SEEN HERE ABOVE THE TUB IN THIS RUSTIC COUNTRY-STYLE BATHROOM. **Right:** THESE CUSTOM-DESIGNED NEOCLASSICAL ARMOIRES WITH OPEN LATTICEWORK PEDIMENTS CREATE A STRONG DESIGN STATEMENT WHEN LIT FROM WITHIN, MAKING THE PEDIMENTS INTO GLOWING CROWNS OF LINEAR PATTERN. RECESSED OVERHEAD LIGHTS SHINING INTO AND AROUND THE ARMOIRES ADD A WARM WHISPER OF ILLUMINATION TO THE SPACE.

Chandeliers and Lamps

Before recessed lighting, track lights, canister lights, and laser lighting, chandeliers and lamps served the primary lighting needs in the home. These traditional lighting solutions remain strong contenders in home design, but in the *best* designs, they are no longer considered the obvious or only answer. Nevertheless, when used in concert with other lighting solutions, chandeliers and lamps can be vital, attractive components in the well-designed room.

While chandeliers and lamps make design statements through the light they emit, they differ from other artificial lighting sources by also making design statements that have nothing to do with light itself but with the style—the appearance—of the lighting vessel. Therein lies their strength, their continued popularity, and their insured longevity in interior design. Because they are decorative as well as functional, chandeliers and lamps can add to the articulation of a room's style in a way no other form of artificial light can.

The good news in decorating is that manufacturers have finally begun to address lamps and chandeliers as design issues, approaching their form and style with the same creativity that is brought to other furnishing design. The basic

Above: For illuminating everyday lifestyle activities such as plopping down in an easy chair or on a sofa with a good book, table lamps provide a time-tested solution. Here, a pair of matched contemporary lamps serves this practical function, while also visually uniting the room. Left: Amid a display of photography, a hand-painted lampshade with delicate silk tassel trim adds elegance, color, and artistic design, while casting intriguing patterns of light and shadow on the photo collection itself.

brass or ginger-jar lamp and the typical crystal chandelier, while remaining classics, have been augmented with a wealth of other lighting designs that encompass all styles, tastes, and colors.

A contemporary room that is essentially architectural in character can now be complemented by Italian-designed metal lamps that are architecture in their own right. A room designed in the popular lodge look—a rustic camp style—can now have its style underscored by a magnificent twig chandelier.

For the collector's home, almost any small antique, from a Staffordshire figurine to an old Chinese wedding basket to a brass horn, can be adapted into a lamp. For the home in which texture is the primary source of design interest, lamps and chandeliers are available in such diverse materials as iron, rattan, wood, bone, glass, and clay. Newly manufactured lamps and chandeliers include period reproductions of every historic type, as well as whimsical creations that are one-of-a-kind.

While a chandelier may not be the best solution for every room in the home, it's hard to imagine a home in which at least one overhead fixture is not appropriate. And it is a stretch to conceive of a home (except, perhaps, one with the most minimalistic design) in which lamplight isn't a practical, as well as aesthetic, strong suit. When choosing the favorite standbys of chandeliers and lamps, consider these lighting solutions as additions to a larger lighting scheme that involves other light sources. Take into account the effect of the light—not all chandeliers or lamps create the same type of lighting—and ensure that the style of the chandeliers and lamps captures the design theme of the space.

Above: TWO CONTEMPORARY CHANDELIERS BRING SPRIGHTLY COLOR TO THE ROOM WITH THEIR STACKED PRIMARY-COLORED DISKS. INSTEAD OF DIRECTING LIGHT DOWNWARD, AS DO MOST CEILING FIXTURES, THESE DIFFUSE LIGHT SIDE-WAYS, CREATING A SOFTER LIGHT SOURCE.

Above: PROOF THAT '50S FURNITURE IS UNDERGOING A REVIVAL, THIS ROOM'S UP-TO-THE-MINUTE RETRO LOOK IS DRAMATIZED BY A MULTI-GLOBED FLOOR LAMP THAT ADDS ESSENTIAL HEIGHT, AS WELL AS LIGHT, TO THE SPACE'S COLLECTION OF LOW-SLUNG FURNISHINGS. VENETIAN BLINDS CREATE THEIR OWN MOODY EFFECT BY DAY WHILE ENHANCING THE '50S THEME.

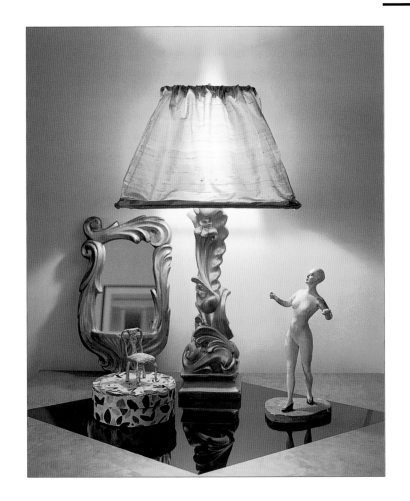

Above left: THIS SMALL TABLE LAMP IS AN *OBJET D'ART* IN ITS OWN RIGHT; WHEN GROUPED WITH OTHER SMALLER ACCESSORIES, IT IS THE FOCAL POINT OF A TABLETOP STILL LIFE, LENDING THE NECESSARY SCALE AND GLOW THAT BALANCE THE ARTFUL COMPOSITION. **Above right:** ONCE A SADLY NEGLECTED AREA OF HOME FURNISHINGS IN TERMS OF INNOVATIVE DESIGN AND MATERIALS, LAMPS TODAY HAVE COME INTO THEIR OWN AS ARENAS OF CREATIVITY, AS PROVEN BY THIS CONTEMPORARY LAMP WITH ITS ARTFUL, TRANSLUCENT PAPER SHADE FORMED IN AN IRREGULAR, TWISTED SHAPE.

Left: HANDCRAFTED LAMPSHADES REPRESENT CLASSIC TURN-OF-THE-CENTURY ARTS AND CRAFTS STYLE IN LIGHTING. THESE CRAFTSMAN LAMPS ARE AUTHENTIC COMPLEMENTS TO A ROOM DECORATED WITH MISSION FURNISHINGS CREATED DURING THE SAME DESIGN MOVEMENT.

Below: NEOCLASSICAL CANDLESTICK LAMPS COMPLEMENT THE NEUTRAL ELEGANCE OF THIS SILVERY BATHROOM, WHILE SERVING THE UTILITARIAN FUNCTION OF ILLUMINATING THE MORNING TOILETTE. LAMPS, COMMONLY FOUND IN BEDROOMS AND LIVING AREAS, ARE SOMEWHAT UNEXPECTED IN THE BATHROOM, THEREBY ADDING GREATER VISUAL INTEREST TO THE SPACE.

Above: VICTORIAN FRINGE CREATES A LIGHTING EFFECT DIFFERENT FROM THAT OF AN UNTRIMMED SHADE, CHANGING THE INTENSITY OF THE LIGHT LIKE A SCREEN. HERE, IT CASTS A SOFT GLOW OVER A COLLECTION OF OLD PHOTOGRAPHS.

Below: A CONTEMPORARY DESK LAMP WITH A COLORED-GLASS GLOBE MAKES A SLEEK DESIGN STATEMENT IN A HOME OFFICE SPACE DOMINATED BY CONTEMPORARY WALL ART.

Above: THE UNIQUE STYLING OF THIS BEDROOM WITH ITS ECLECTIC COLLECTIBLES WOULD BE ILL SERVED BY A BLAND LAMP. THE RIGHT SOLUTION IS ONE THAT ENHANCES THE ROOM'S INDIVIDUALITY, LIKE THIS CERAMIC BEDSIDE LAMP WITH ITS TURBANED-HEAD BASE AND TEXTURED PAPER SHADE.

Above: An Art Nouveau bronze figurine rising up from a newel post serves as an arresting lamp to shed light on the ascent up the stairs. **Left:** Among the main draws of lamps are the unlimited possibilities they offer for creative expression. Almost any favorite collectible can be adapted and wired to function as a lamp, as illustrated by this dressmaker's dummy turned chairside lamp.

Above left: A LASSOING COWBOY BECOMES A CONVERSATIONAL ITEM WHEN TRANSFORMED INTO THE BASE OF A TABLE LAMP IN A SOUTHWESTERN-STYLE ROOM. **Above right:** PAPER SCONCES PATTERNED WITH INKY DINOSAURS CAST A SURREAL GLOW ON THE WALL. THE BLACK PICTORIAL DESIGN STANDS IN STRIKING CONTRAST TO THE GOLDEN BACKGROUND. **Right:** WITH ITS ELONGATED IRON BASE, THIS FLOOR LAMP REPRESENTS THE BEST OF POPULAR OLD WEST DESIGN AS A MELDING OF RUSTIC TEXTURE AND CLASSIC NATIVE AMERICAN MOTIFS.

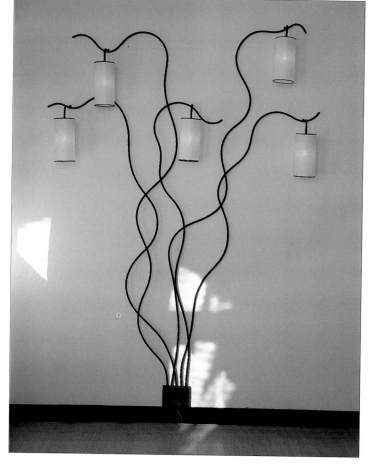

Below: AS MUCH A CONTEMPORARY SCULPTURE AS A LIGHTING FIXTURE, THIS TREE LAMP FEATURES SINEWY IRON BRANCHES BEARING GOLDEN CYLINDERS OF LIGHT.

Above: A CONTEMPORARY CLASSIC, THIS ARCHITECTURAL LAMP COMPLEMENTS THE ROOM'S MODERN DESIGN AND ARCHITECTURE WHILE ALSO SERVING THE PRACTICAL FUNCTION OF PROVIDING A GOOD READING LIGHT.

Left: IN A BOLD, CONTEMPORARY ROOM IN WHICH EACH FURNISHING HAS A DISTINCTIVE, SCULPTURAL FORM, PAPER LANTERNS PLAY AN INTEGRAL ROLE IN ARTICULATING THE DESIGN THEME WITH THEIR GEOMETRIC SHAPES AND STARK SIMPLICITY.

Above left: AN ANTIQUE ART-GLASS CHANDELIER OF SUBSTANTIAL SCALE LENDS PERIOD CHARM TO A STATELY ROOM, WHILE ALSO SERVING TO DEFINE THE ROOM'S FOCAL POINT—THE EXQUISITE INLAID MARBLE TABLE. **Above right:** A PAIR OF CANDLESTICK LAMPS BRINGS UNDERSTATED ELEGANCE TO A DECORATIVE CONSOLE TABLE CAPPED WITH AN OPULENTLY CARVED MIRROR IN WHICH CAN BE SEEN THE REFLECTION OF A GLOWING CHANDELIER. **Right:** DARK METAL STAR SCONCES FORCE LIGHT BEHIND AND AROUND THEIR DISTINCTIVE SHAPE, CREATING A CHARMING HALO EFFECT. THE ROOM ALSO UTILIZES DOWN-LIGHTS FOR FOCUSING UPON THE ART AND THE ARCHITECTURAL MIRROR.

Left: AS WITH OTHER ASPECTS OF DECORATING, ATTENTION TO DETAIL IN LIGHTING REWARDS THE EFFORT WITH GREAT RESULTS. HERE, ANTIQUE GLASS GLOBES WITH DELICATE, LACY PATTERNS IMBUE A CHANDELIER WITH A RICH, ERSTWHILE CHARACTER. **Below:** AS LIGHTING BECOMES AN INCREASINGLY POPULAR AREA FOR CREATIVITY IN DESIGN, SOME UNIQUE FIXTURES ARE AVAILABLE. FASHIONED FROM KITCHEN EQUIPMENT, BEADS, AND OTHER UNUSUAL ELEMENTS, THIS WITTY AND FUNCTIONAL CHANDELIER PROVIDES THE ROOM WITH BOTH LIGHT AND A SENSE OF FUN.

Left: THE SOPHISTICATED LIGHTING PLAN IN THIS DINING ROOM INCLUDES A RECESSED DOWN-LIGHT IN THE NICHE AND SPOTS THAT FOCUS LIGHT DOWN FROM THE CEILING, BUT THE OUTSTANDING FEATURE IS THE CUSTOM-MADE MEXICAN CHANDELIER. ITS ARMATURE HAS BEEN SOFTENED BY A GRAPEVINE WRAPPING, WHILE ITS UNIQUE LAMPS ARE MADE OF STAINLESS-STEEL MESH MOLDED INTO FLAME-LIKE FORMS. THE RESULT IS A WONDERFUL INTERPLAY OF LIGHT AND SHADOW THAT BOTH PROVIDES ILLUMINATION AND CREATES A DRAMATIC YET INTIMATE MOOD.

Above: FOR SOME ROOMS, THE INCOMPARABLE ELEGANCE OF A TRADITIONAL CHANDELIER

REMAINS THE PERFECT CHOICE. IN THIS GRAND CIRCULAR FOYER SPANNING TWO

STORIES, THE CHANDELIER IS THE *PIÈCE DE RÉSISTANCE.* **Right:** IN THIS OPULENT LIVING

ROOM, A FINE CRYSTAL CHANDELIER MAKES A STATEMENT OF REFINED GRACE.

Above: LIKE THE CABIN OF A HOT-AIR BALLOON, THE PETITE LIGHTING PORTION OF THIS OVERHEAD FIXTURE IS SUSPENDED BY SHEER WHIMSY, ENHANCING THE ROOM'S APPEALING COTTAGE CHARM. **Right:** A FRINGED TIFFANY-STYLE GLASS VICTORIAN CHANDELIER BRINGS TURN-OF-THE-CENTURY WARMTH TO A HEAVILY PANELED DINING AREA THAT FEATURES A LACE-DRAPED TABLE.

Above: THE LIGHTING TREATMENT FOR THIS ELONGATED ISLAND BAR IS A VARIATION ON OVERHEAD CHANDELIERS: INSTEAD OF A SINGLE CHANDELIER, THREE SMALL CONTEMPORARY LIGHTS DANGLE CLOSE TO THE WORK SPACE FROM LONG RIBBONS OF CABLE.

Above: DESPITE ITS ELECTRIFIED-CANDLE FORM, THERE IS NOTHING TRADITIONAL ABOUT THIS DINING ROOM CHANDELIER, WITH ITS RUSTIC, FREE-FORM TWIG DESIGN THAT IS AN IDEAL COMPANION TO THE TABLE BASE BELOW.

Above: RATHER THAN OVERWHELMING WITH OPULENCE, THIS GRACEFUL ANTIQUE CHANDELIER CONVEYS A SPIRIT OF RESTRAINED FINERY WITH ITS DELICATE FORM, SCALE, AND MATERIALS. **Left:** THE KEY TO THE EFFECTIVENESS OF THIS TURN-OF-THE-CENTURY CRAFTSMAN CHANDELIER LIES IN ITS UNEXPECTED PLACEMENT JUST INCHES ABOVE THE DINING TABLE—A CHOICE THAT REVEALS THE REWARDS OF PLANNING AND A WILLINGNESS TO BEND RULES.

Above: SUSPENDED FROM IRON CHAINS AND OUTFITTED WITH APPROPRIATE LIGHTING HARD-
WARE, AN OLD WAGON WHEEL MAKES A UNIQUELY APT CHANDELIER FOR A ROOM DECORATED IN AN
AMERICAN SOUTHWEST STYLE. **Right:** AN ENORMOUSLY HIGH CEILING REQUIRES A LONG CABLE
TO BRING A CHANDELIER DOWN TO HUMAN LEVEL, WHERE THE CONTEMPORARY FIXTURE
CAN SHED LIGHT ON A DINING TABLE.

SOURCES

DESIGNERS

(page 6)
Nancy Goslee Power
Los Angeles, CA
(310) 396-4765

(pages 9; 15; 21, right; 41)
Nick Berman
Los Angeles, CA
(310) 476-6242

(page 13)
Benjamin Nutter, architect
Topsfield, MA
(508) 887-9836

(pages 16; 24, left; 27,
  right; 31)
Brian Murphy
Santa Monica, CA
(310) 459-0955

(page 17)
Steven Ehrlich
Santa Monica, CA
(310) 828-6700

(page 19; front cover)
Steven Chase
Palm Springs, CA
(619) 324-4602

(page 20, left)
Schwartz/Silver Architects
Boston, MA
(617) 542-6650

(page 20, right)
Bill Spink
Spink, Inc.
New York, NY
(212) 226-8022

(page 23)
Allie Chang Paul
Santa Monica, CA
(310) 459-1081

(page 24, right)
Michael Berman
Los Angeles, CA
(213) 655-9813

(page 25, right)
Margaret Helfand Architects
New York, NY
(212) 779-7260

(page 26)
Lou Goodman
New York, NY
(212) 243-4236

(page 29)
William Ku
Rochester Hills, MI
(313) 650-1300

(page 30)
Gayle Reynolds, ASID
Lexington, MA
(617) 863-5169

(page 33)
Robert Wine
Birmingham, MI
(810) 642-2317

(page 34, left)
Tom O'Toole
New York, NY
(212) 348-0639

(page 36)
Moore, Rubel, and Yudell
Mill Valley, CA
(213) 450-1400

(page 38, left)
Francois deMenil, Architect, P.C.
New York, NY
(212) 779-3400

(page 38, right)
Margot Alofsin
Los Angeles, CA
(310) 395-8008

(page 39)
Anthony P. Browne, Inc.
Washington, D.C.
(202) 333-1903

(page 40)
Brenda Speight
Fredricksburg, TX

(page 42)
Andrew Reczkowski
Chelsea, MA
(617) 884-4365

(pages 43; 47, left & right)
C & J Katz Studio
Boston, MA
(617) 367-0537

(page 44)
Peter Shire
Los Angeles, CA
(213) 662-5385

(page 45)
Neil Korpinen
Los Angeles, CA
(213) 661-9861

(page 48, left)
J.S. Brown Design
Pasadena, CA
(818) 304-9701

(page 48, right)
The Little River Inn
Little River, CA
(707) 937-5942

(page 49, left)
Louann Bauer
San Francisco, CA
(415) 621-7262

(pages 52, left & right; 53)
Truewest Designs
Clackamas, OR
(503) 658-8753

(page 54)
Stamberg Aferiat Architecture
New York, NY
(212) 255-4173

(page 55, right)
fixture by Jean Royere

(page 56, left)
Shana Lev
New York, NY
(212) 496-8087

(page 57)
Jeffrey Lincoln
Locust Valley, NY
(516) 759-6100

(page 58)
David Livingston Interior Design
San Francisco, CA
(415) 392-2465

(page 59, right)
fixture by Patrice Butler

(page 62)
Debra Jones
Los Angeles, CA
(310) 476-1824

(page 64)
George Padilla
Pasadena, CA
(213) 254-0636

(page 68)
Janet Lohman Design
Los Angeles, CA
(310) 471-3955

PHOTOGRAPHY CREDITS

© Peter Aaron/Esto
   Photographics: p. 36

© Balthazar Korab: pp. 29, 33

© James Brett: pp. 21 left,
   25 left

© Grey Crawford: pp. 9, 15,
   17, 21 right, 24 right, 27
   left, 37, 41, 45, 64, 65,
   66, 69

© Mark Darley/Esto
   Photographics: p. 26

© Derrick & Love: p. 20 right

© Feliciano: pp. 55 left, 60, 67

© Scott Frances/Esto
   Photographics: pp. 50, 61

© Michael Garland: pp. 22 left
   & right, 23, 48 left & right,
   56 right, 59 left

© Mick Hales: p. 46

© Image/Dennis Krukowski:
   pp. 34 left & right, 39,
   40, 57

© David Livingston: pp. 10, 18,
   49 left, 58

© Mark Lohman: p. 68

© Peter Paige: p. 56 left

© Paul Rocheleau: p. 63

© Eric Roth: pp. 2, 12, 13, 30,
   35 left & right, 42, 43, 47
   left & right

© Richard Sexton: p. 51

© Tim Street-Porter: pp. 6, 16,
   19, 24 left, 27 right, 28,
   31, 38 left, 44, 55 right,
   59 right, 62

Courtesy of Truewest Designs:
   pp. 52 left & right, 53

© Paul Warchol: pp. 20 left,
   25 right, 38 right, 49 right,
   54

INDEX